American values, one story at a time.

Larry Elder

Clarence Thomas — A Justice for All

Illustrations by Dan Burr

Text copyright © Heroes of Liberty Inc., 2023

Illustrations copyright Heroes of Liberty Inc., 2023

1216 Broadway, New York, NY 10001

All rights reserved. No part of this book may be reproduced or transmitted in any form or by any means, electronic or mechanical, including photocopying, recording, or by any information storage and retrieval system without written permission from the publisher.

Heroes of Liberty Inc.
1216 Broadway, New York, NY 10001

Find more heroes to read about on:

WWW.HEROESOFLIBERTY.COM

Clarence Thomas

A JUSTICE FOR ALL

Clarence Thomas

Clarence Thomas made history as a fierce defender of free speech and as the second black American to become a justice on the Supreme Court of the United States. The Supreme Court is the head of the Judicial Branch and is made up of nine justices who serve lifetime appointments. It is the highest court in the land and makes the final decisions on legal matters. Justice Thomas is the longest serving member on the Supreme Court today.

Clarence's life began in poverty in Pinpoint, Georgia. Though he could barely read, his grandfather taught him what it means to be a good man; to work hard, and not make excuses for hardships in life. Instead of being angry about the inequalities he faced as a young boy in the segregated South, Clarence Thomas devoted his life to the promise of the Declaration of Independence of the United States that ALL MEN ARE CREATED EQUAL.

YALE

LUX ET VERITAS

GRADUATED YALE UNIVERSITY
LAW SCHOOL, 1974
NEW HAVEN, CT

CHAIRMAN OF EQUAL
EMPLOYMENT OPPORTUNITY
COMMISSION, 1982-1990
WASHINGTON, DC

SWORN IN AS 106TH JUSTICE
OF UNITED STATES SUPREME
COURT — OCT. 23, 1991
WHITE HOUSE, WASHINGTON, DC

CT

MO

GA

ASSISTANT ATTORNEY
GENERAL, 1974-1977
CAPITOL BUILDING,
JEFFERSON CITY, MO

BORN JUNE 23, 1948
PINPOINT, GA

The Justices of the Supreme Court work very hard, reviewing the most important legal cases that affect all Americans. When the Supreme Court goes on recess, Clarence Thomas and his wife, Ginni, like to get away from Washington, D.C. and enjoy the sights of our beautiful country: the Grand Canyon, Mount Rushmore, and hundreds of places in between. The Thomases hop in their 40-foot RV and, along the way, they meet ordinary Americans.

Justices meet a lot of important people at their job: presidents, senators, and other attorneys. But they are on the Supreme Court to serve all Americans. Justice Thomas believes it is very important to be in touch with ordinary citizens so he can learn firsthand what is on their minds, what they hope for, and what they worry about, so that the Court may better serve them.

One time, when the Thomases made a stop at a Walmart in Georgia, a truck driver said, "Did anybody ever tell you that you look like Justice Clarence Thomas?" Justice Thomas smiled and said, "Oh, yeah. It happens all the time."

Imagine that man's surprise when he learned he was speaking to the real Justice Thomas! It's not every day that you get to speak to a Justice of the U.S. Supreme Court.

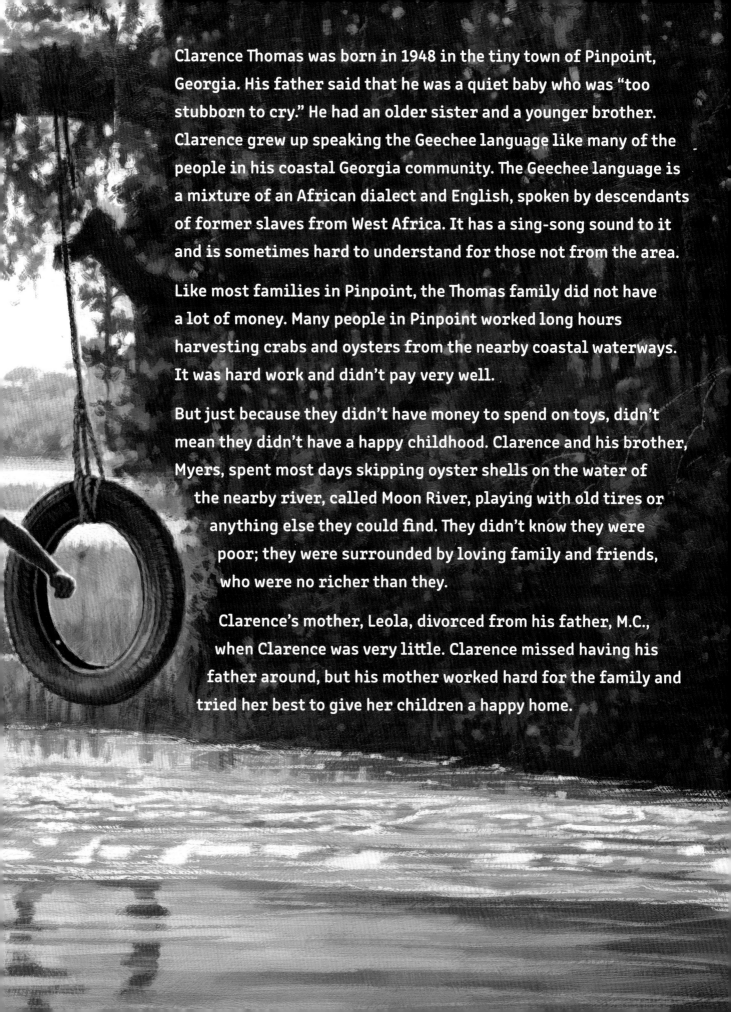

Clarence Thomas was born in 1948 in the tiny town of Pinpoint, Georgia. His father said that he was a quiet baby who was "too stubborn to cry." He had an older sister and a younger brother. Clarence grew up speaking the Geechee language like many of the people in his coastal Georgia community. The Geechee language is a mixture of an African dialect and English, spoken by descendants of former slaves from West Africa. It has a sing-song sound to it and is sometimes hard to understand for those not from the area.

Like most families in Pinpoint, the Thomas family did not have a lot of money. Many people in Pinpoint worked long hours harvesting crabs and oysters from the nearby coastal waterways. It was hard work and didn't pay very well.

But just because they didn't have money to spend on toys, didn't mean they didn't have a happy childhood. Clarence and his brother, Myers, spent most days skipping oyster shells on the water of the nearby river, called Moon River, playing with old tires or anything else they could find. They didn't know they were poor; they were surrounded by loving family and friends, who were no richer than they.

Clarence's mother, Leola, divorced from his father, M.C., when Clarence was very little. Clarence missed having his father around, but his mother worked hard for the family and tried her best to give her children a happy home.

One day, disaster struck: the Thomases came home to find their house had burned down to the ground. Myers and a cousin had been playing with matches and accidentally caused the fire. Nothing was left. Leola had no choice but to take her two boys and move to the bigger city of Savannah, where she could find work. They could only afford to live in a dilapidated, crowded apartment building. The worst part was that they had to share with everyone else one smelly, broken toilet that was outside. It was terrible.

Clarence and Myers did not like living in Savannah. Their mother sometimes earned only pennies and they had very little to eat—he and Myers were growing boys and were always hungry. In the winter, their room was cold and there was no running water in their apartment. During the day, when Leola was at work, Clarence and his little brother walked around downtown Savannah by themselves, even though they were only seven and four. They had no one to watch over them.

Sometimes they would walk to Forsyth Park, a beautiful green park with a big fountain in the middle that spurted out fresh water. But because they were black, they were not allowed to walk in the center of the park. Clarence did not like that or think it was fair.

Leola worried about her boys being left alone too much while she worked as a maid. So she was glad when her father and stepmother, who lived in Savannah, offered to have the boys live with them. Leola felt it would be better for the boys. And so one day she came home and gave the boys a paper grocery bag. She told them to put everything they owned in the bag because they were going to go live with their grandparents. They had so few things that the bag wasn't even full.

Clarence's grandfather, Myers Anderson, was a very serious man. He sat the boys down for a talk and told them that he was happy that they were there, but they had to follow the rules. "Rule number one," he said, "Grandma is always right. Rule number two: The door swings in and out. Right now it swings in, but if you misbehave it will swing out."

Though the house was a simple one, to Clarence and Myers it felt like a palace. They had never experienced such a wonderful place! There was plenty of food, a brand-new kitchen, running water, and a toilet that flushed! They would flush the toilet every time they passed by just for fun.

Grandfather Myers had only gone to school through third grade because he had to go to work and earn money for his family. He could barely read himself, but he wanted more for his grandsons. He clearly understood that education was the key to success, so he enrolled the boys in a Catholic school run by Irish nuns. At that time schools in the South were still segregated; white and black children could not go to the same school. St. Benedict's was for black children only.

The school was clean and orderly, and the Irish nuns loved the students and did not like the unfair treatment of blacks. But they were also strict. They expected a great deal out of their pupils. After taking an achievement test, one of the nuns, Sister Mary Virgilius, realized that Clarence was very talented and could achieve much more. She called him to her desk and handed him the test he had done well on. She said, "You lazy thing, you! You are a smart boy. You can do as well on other tests, and I expect you to!" Clarence lowered his eyes. He was proud that he had done well on the test, but ashamed that he hadn't been trying hard in school. He promised he would work harder from now on.

Grandpa Myers also believed in the importance of hard work. So, every day, when school got out at 2:30 p.m., Clarence and Myers rushed home to get dressed for work. They were on their grandfather's truck by 3, helping deliver oil and ice all around Savannah. In those days, most people didn't have electric refrigerators and needed big chunks of ice to keep their food cold. In the winter, they needed oil delivered to heat their homes.

During the summer and weekends, they would work on the family farm. It was hard work: sawing trees, plowing fields with an old stubborn horse, cleaning stinky fish. Grandpa Myers quoted the Bible often and told the boys they should work "from sun to sun"—from sunrise to sunset. When the boys would say, "We can't do this, it's too hard!", he would get a twinkle in his eye and say, "Old Man Can't is dead. I helped bury him." It was his way of saying: don't ever say you can't do something just because it's hard.

Clarence called Grandpa Myers "Daddy," because he was like a father to him. Living up to the old man's demands was very hard. But Clarence knew his grandfather did it out of love. He wanted his grandchildren to develop a strong, honest character.

Clarence loved going to church with Daddy. He especially loved the musical Gregorian chants and prayers said at Mass. He thought God might be calling him to become a Catholic priest and wanted to go to a seminary for high school. A seminary is a place where young men who are discerning the priesthood begin their religious training.

Grandpa Myers did not like the idea, but he agreed to let him go on the condition that if he started down this path, he would follow it to the end. Clarence promised he would not quit.

So, at 16 years old, Clarence entered St. John Vianney Seminary on the Isle of Hope in Savannah, Georgia. He was one of only a few black seminarians and sometimes felt very lonely. The head of the seminary told Clarence that he needed to learn to speak standard English in order to succeed. You see, though Clarence had worked hard in school to speak well, the Geechee dialect was still noticeable when he spoke.

He studied more than just about anyone and felt he had to make perfect grades. Once, he made a 98% on a test and still said, "That's not good enough."

Clarence was not happy at the seminary, but
he did not want to break his promise to Daddy.
So he kept on working hard at his studies.

In those years, Dr. Martin Luther King, Jr. was
working hard to change how black people were
treated, especially in the South. He was a Baptist
preacher and believed that Christians should stand
up for equal rights for all people, no matter the
color of their skin. Some people thought violence
was the way to make that happen. Dr. King said
absolutely not. He preached nonviolent protest.
He believed in the United States Constitution,
and in the teachings of Jesus Christ, and thought
we must work peacefully to make America live
up to its promise. Clarence admired Dr. King.

On April 4, 1968, Dr. Martin Luther King, Jr. was shot and killed in Memphis, Tennessee. Clarence was heartbroken. Some of the seminarians did not care and some even said racist things like they were glad Dr. King had died. Clarence was hurt and angry and decided to leave the seminary and go home.

But what awaited him at home gave him no comfort. Daddy sat him down and reminded him, "I told you the door swings in and it swings out. You promised not to quit the seminary, but you did not keep your word. So now the door swings out." Clarence left his grandfather's house the next day and went to live with his mother. He was hurt and lost without his grandfather's direction, but also angry that Daddy didn't understand why he had to leave the seminary.

Clarence had to make new plans. One of the nuns who had taught Clarence suggested that he apply to the College of the Holy Cross in Worcester, Massachusetts. No one in his family had ever gone to college, so it was exciting when he was accepted and traveled north for the first time. But Clarence was still angry about Martin Luther King, Jr.'s death and decided to take part in the founding of a black students' union to fight for racial equality.

Unlike Martin Luther King, Jr., many in his new circle were leftist political radicals who believed in using violence to get what they wanted. Most of them did not believe in God and did not like America. One night, Clarence Thomas joined an angry mob that was protesting America's involvement in a war against communism, far away in a country called Vietnam. The protest turned into a violent riot. Buildings were set on fire, rocks were thrown, and many people got hurt.

Back at Holy Cross, Clarence was deeply shaken by all the violence, and deeply regretted participating in it. He started to think that his leftist friends were going about things the wrong way. He knew Daddy would be disappointed in what he had done.

Clarence went to the chapel at school; it was the first time he had prayed in two years. He promised God that if He would take the anger out of his heart, he would try to be better.

Young Clarence Thomas graduated from Holy Cross and was accepted to Yale, one of the top law schools in America. Since God had helped take the anger out of his heart, Clarence kept his promise and worked extra hard to do well in law school. His life began to make sense and he was happy. He got married to Kathy Ambush and had a son named Jamal. He loved being with Jamal and having fun with him. He also tried to teach him some of the important lessons he had learned from his grandfather.

After graduation, Clarence Thomas worked
for the Attorney General of Missouri, who
was a Republican, although Clarence had
thus far always voted for Democrats.

When his boss was elected Senator, he asked Clarence
Thomas to come to Washington, D.C. with him to
work in the Senate on Capitol Hill. It was while
working in the Senate that Clarence Thomas saw
the differences between the two political parties
more clearly. A man named Ronald Reagan, a former
actor and governor of California, was running to be
president of the United States for the Republicans.

Reagan had once been a Democrat too, before he came to think that it was a mistake to believe that the government can solve people's problems for them. People know what's best for themselves. If the government makes their decisions for them, it only makes their problems worse. Clarence Thomas had never voted for a Republican before, but he liked that Reagan wanted to stop the government from making too many laws that burdened people—especially poor people.

Ronald Reagan won the presidency in a landslide! It was the beginning of the Reagan Revolution that ushered in years of prosperity and pride in the United States.

Clarence Thomas wanted to learn more about President Reagan's views. So, he decided to attend a conference on the subject, the Fairmont Conference in San Francisco, California. A famous economist, Thomas Sowell, spoke at the conference about how blacks in America shouldn't rely on the government to solve their problems, because this will only prevent them from becoming independent and prosperous. He said that, while being a victim is tempting, it actually keeps you from doing great things. If you sink into self-pity, you can't help yourself. Professor Sowell said many things that reminded Clarence Thomas of how wise his grandfather was, despite his lack of education. Like Grandpa Myers, Thomas Sowell knew that we don't really appreciate the things we have if we haven't worked to achieve them ourselves.

The Fairmont Conference turned out to be a pivotal event in Clarence Thomas's life. He met other black Americans who thought like he did, and he realized he was not alone. He decided he would use his voice to help empower all Americans to reach their potential.

President Ronald Reagan liked how Clarence Thomas thought about the role of government in people's lives and asked him to be in charge of making sure that there was no discrimination against people trying to work in America. He was excited about the role, but many people did not like that Clarence Thomas was now working for a Republican. Some people called him a traitor to his race.

That hurt, especially when it came from black leaders he had once looked up to. Of course, the opposite was true: Clarence Thomas did not turn his back on black people. It was just that he thought Dr. Sowell's ideas would help them more. Like Dr. Sowell, he believed that all people—regardless of color—can only be truly happy when they take responsibility for their own lives. It would have been easier to change his views and be popular with the black leaders, but Clarence Thomas wanted to offer real help, even if it would make him unpopular. He refused to be intimidated.

All was going well in Washington, D.C., but then Clarence got the sad news that his beloved grandfather had died. His step-grandmother died shortly after. He went to Georgia for their funerals. They had been like a father and mother to him. He was heartbroken. He cried and cried. He had been so busy with his career that he hadn't had much time to see them. But he knew he was doing what Daddy had taught him: work hard, be honest, and never give up. Daddy would have been proud. He was sure of that.

When he got back to Washington, he was still sad. He wondered what life really meant, as people often do when they lose someone they love. One night, as he walked outside in the quiet darkness, he asked himself, "Is there anything you are willing to die for, Clarence?" He looked up and saw the brightly lit white dome of the United States Capitol in the distance. His heart swelled and he knew; he believed in the principles of liberty enshrined in the Constitution of the United States of America, and in the words of our Declaration of Independence: that "all men are created equal, that they are endowed by their Creator with certain unalienable rights, and that among these are life, liberty, and the pursuit of happiness." Clarence Thomas believed in those words so strongly that yes, he would die for them if he had to.

Clarence Thomas did such good work at his job for the Reagan Administration, that he was appointed by the next Republican President George H.W. Bush to be a federal judge in Washington, D.C. He was approved by the Senate and enjoyed working with other judges, including the famous Judge Ruth Bader Ginsburg, beside whom he would later work at the Supreme Court. They differed on their legal opinions, but they both believed they could disagree without being disagreeable. Judge Ginsburg appreciated that Judge Thomas shared her belief in being civil and working hard.

But he was a bit lonely. His marriage to Jamal's mother had sadly ended in divorce. He prayed for years that God would send him someone to share his life with. And He did. At a conference he met Virginia "Ginni" Lamp. They shared many of the same beliefs in God and the United States and began dating. Clarence and Ginni were married in 1987.

There are nine justices on the U.S. Supreme Court. When one retires or dies, the President gets to appoint a new justice. According to the Constitution, the Senate must give "advice and consent" to such appointments, so they only go through if the Senate approves.

In 1990, Thurgood Marshall, the first black American to serve as a Supreme Court justice, died. President George H.W. Bush nominated Clarence Thomas to fill his position. But many leftist activists, including black activists, were against him. They were afraid that his belief in smaller government would be an obstacle to their plans to have the federal government run people's lives for them.

Once again, black activists blamed him unjustly for betraying the black community, while he believed his way would help them more.

To Clarence Thomas, it felt like when he was little and wasn't allowed to walk through Forsyth Park in Savannah just because he was black. Now, it wasn't about walking through a park; it was about some people believing he should not be allowed to think a different way just because he was black. Clarence Thomas would not allow them to bully him into backing down from what he knew was right. He would walk tall and not back down from his beliefs.

During the confirmation hearings, led by then-Senator Joe Biden, many of the Democrat senators tried to find fault with Clarence Thomas's legal opinions. But they failed. He would not say how he would decide on legal issues which were important to them. They were getting frustrated that they could not find a reason to reject him.

Then, a woman named Anita Hill, who used to work with him, came to the U.S. Senate Judiciary Committee to testify that Clarence Thomas had acted very rudely toward her while they worked together. Her allegations were thoroughly investigated but no proof was found. In fact, many others who had worked with Clarence Thomas testified that he had always been kind and considerate.

It was a terrible time for Judge Thomas. His good name was being tarnished on TV. Every morning, he and Ginni would pray to put on the armor of God before they entered the Senate committee room. He realized that his enemies were not only the old-time racists, but also the modern liberals, who thought they knew what blacks should think. Many hoped he would quit. But Clarence Thomas remembered Grandpa's words when things got hard working on the farm: "Give out, but don't give up." He would not quit. In the end, his nomination passed and he was confirmed to the Supreme Court.

Mr. BIDEN

Mr.

Clarence Thomas was sworn in as the 106th Justice of the U.S. Supreme Court on October 23, 1991. He has now been serving more than thirty years on the Court.

It is a great honor to be an attorney and argue a case before the U.S. Supreme Court. It can also be very intimidating. Justice Thomas likes to listen to the attorneys instead of asking a lot of questions. He believes they have worked hard to make their cases, and they deserve his full attention. When all is said by both parties, Justice Thomas makes his decision based on the Constitution.

He is still a hard worker. Though he is only one of nine justices, he has written almost a third of all decisions made by the Supreme Court during his time.

Justice Clarence Thomas is known as a fierce defender of the First Amendment to the Constitution, the amendment that guarantees the right to free speech. It is easy to defend the right of people you agree with to speak their mind. But Justice Thomas believes we must also protect the right of people we don't agree with to voice their views. Because, though we may not know it now, it may one day turn out that they were right and we were wrong. God only knows. And we are not God

Justice Clarence Thomas often works until the late hours at the Supreme Court, writing legal decisions that will affect Americans for years to come. Above his desk sits a bust of his grandfather, with the inscription, "Old Man Can't is dead. I helped bury him." It makes him smile to remember Daddy's words and reminds him of the importance of working hard and never giving up, even when things are difficult.

Though he is one of the most powerful people in America, he knows the name of every person who works at the Supreme Court building, from janitors to security guards, and often the names of their family members. Even justices who usually disagree with him on many cases think Justice Thomas is one of the kindest, most caring, and thoughtful people they know.

Each year, Justice Thomas mentors young lawyers from all across America who clerk for him at the Supreme Court. He passes on the lessons he learned from his grandfather: hard work, integrity, and love for the United States and its exceptional Constitution.

7

INTERESTING FACTS ABOUT

Clarence Thomas

HE IS AN ATHLETE AND RAN THE MARINE CORPS
MARATHON (26.2 MILES) IN WASHINGTON, D.C.

THOUGH HE NEVER LIVED IN TEXAS,
JUSTICE THOMAS IS AN AVID FAN OF
THE DALLAS COWBOYS.

HE PLAYED INTRAMURAL FOOTBALL AT
YALE LAW SCHOOL.

HE BECAME THE SECOND BLACK AMERICAN TO SERVE ON THE SUPREME COURT.

PORTRAITS OF BOOKER T. WASHINGTON AND FREDERICK DOUGLASS HANG IN HIS OFFICE IN THE SUPREME COURT.

THESE ARE THE SAME PICTURES THAT HUNG ON THE WALLS OF THE PUBLIC LIBRARY WHERE YOUNG CLARENCE LEARNED TO READ.

IN 1999, JUSTICE THOMAS BECAME THE FIRST SUPREME COURT JUSTICE TO SERVE AS GRAND MARSHAL OF THE DAYTONA 500 NASCAR RACE.

"I'd grown up fearing the lynch mobs of the Ku Klux Klan; as an adult I was starting to wonder if I'd been afraid of the wrong white people all along – where I was being pursued not by bigots in white robes, but by left-wing zealots draped in flowing sanctimony."

Clarence Thomas

"Good manners will open doors that the best education cannot."

Clarence Thomas

"I don't believe in quotas. America was founded on a philosophy of individual rights, not group rights."

Clarence Thomas

"I grew up in a religious environment, and I'm proud of it. I was going to be a priest; I'm proud of it. And I thank God I believe in God, or I would probably be enormously angry right now."

Clarence Thomas

Check out the previous books in the Heroes of Liberty series

Ronald Reagan

IT'S MORNING IN AMERICA

BY CHRISTINE O'HARE

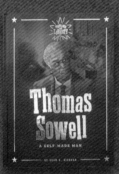

Thomas Sowell

A SELF MADE MAN

BY SEAN A. NICKSON

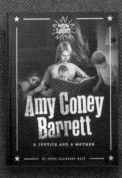

Amy Coney Barrett

A JUSTICE AND A MOTHER

BY JOYCE CLAIBORNE WELT

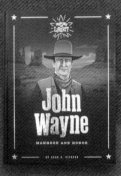

John Wayne

MANHOOD AND HONOR

BY SEAN A. NICKSON

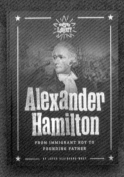

Alexander Hamilton

FROM IMMIGRANT BOY TO FOUNDING FATHER

BY JOYCE CLAIBORNE WELT

Margaret Thatcher

THE IRON LADY

BY CHRISTINE O'HARE

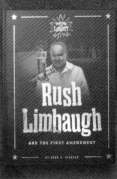

Rush Limbaugh

AND THE FIRST AMENDMENT

BY SEAN A. NICKSON

Douglas MacArthur

DUTY, HONOR, COUNTRY

BY SEAN B. GIBSON

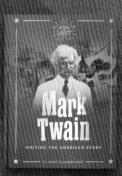

Mark Twain

WRITING THE AMERICAN STORY

BY JOYCE CLAIBORNE WEST

Clara Barton

THE ANGEL OF
THE BATTLEFIELD

BY CHRISTINE O'HARE

Winston Churchill

COURAGE IN THE
FACE OF DARKNESS

BY JOYCE CLAIBORNE WEST

Harriet Tubman

FAITH AND DELIVERANCE

CHRISTINE O'HARE

John Paul II

BE NOT AFRAID!

BY RICK SANTORUM

Elon Musk

OCCUPY MARS

BY STEPHEN L. RISE